WOMEN VOTE
RED

WOMEN VOTE
RED

RUTH SNOW

Liberty Hill Publishing

Liberty Hill Publishing
2301 Lucien Way #415
Maitland, FL 32751
407.339.4217
www.libertyhillpublishing.com

Printed in the United States of America.

ISBN-13: 978-1-5456-7676-9

To all women who want to keep America great!

Dedication

To my Dedo and Baba who understood the privilege of becoming US citizens; my dad who taught me to appreciate freedom in his intelligent, humble way; my mother who taught me the value of hard work; my sisters who teach me how to respectfully disagree; and my brother who keeps the conversation going about generations past and the generations yet to come.

To my husband, Dan, without your wisdom, love and support, this book would not have been accomplished.

Contents

Dedication. vii

Chapter One - Election 2016 1

Chapter 2 - The "Uneducated" in America. 7

Chapter Three - The Vote. 17

Chapter Four - Fear of "free" speech. 33

Chapter Five - Immigration. 41

Chapter Six - Sanctity of Life 55

Chapter Seven - The Women BESIDE Trump . . 61

Chapter Eight - 2020 Election 69

About the Author. 77
References 79

Chapter One

Election 2016

P resident Donald J. Trump's final words exiting his campaign run for the 2016 election:

Just imagine what our country could accomplish if we started working together as one people, under one God, saluting one American flag. I'm asking you to dream big because with your vote we are just hours away from the change you've been waiting for your entire life. So to every parent who dreams for their child and to every child who dreams for their future I say these words to you tonight. I am with you. I will fight for you and I will win for you. I promise. (Holt 2017)

Let's go back and relive the excitement of the 2016 presidential election evening — remember, the doubt of Trump being elected? The slow unraveling of his popularity among thirty states voicing the will of the American people! Trump won states that have traditionally swung blue — states like Wisconsin, where the last Republican win was in 1984, and Pennsylvania, where the last Republican win was in 1988. (Huange 2016) On election night, he transformed those blue states to red! His hard work and revival of the middle class secured the swing states of Florida, Ohio, and North Carolina. (Gregg 2017) What a success! What an evening it was, when middle-class citizens used their voice to elect a man outside of political graces, a man who demonstrated resilience, work ethic, and straight talk on the campaign trail, and a president-elect who wasn't owned and couldn't be bought – the 45th President of the United States, Donald J. Trump!

Barack Obama and many other Democrats said that Donald J. Trump would not become the president of the United States. After proving to the Democrats, America, and the rest of world that he did have the support of the American people to be commander in chief, the response from the Democratic Party was that of shock and disbelief. Journalist Jeff Jarvis responded with "I'll say it: This is the victory of the uneducated and the uninformed. Now more than ever that looks impossible to fix. They now rule." (Glum 2017) Americans took to social media in a frenzy to vent and express themselves. One twitter comment referred to the newly elected president as "the 9/11 of all presidents. You broke America, you living joke." (Glum 2017) MSNBC host, Rachel Maddow helped Americans begin the hate speech by offering her opinion to the public "You're not having a terrible, terrible dream. Also, you're not dead, and you haven't gone to hell. This is your life now." (Glum 2017.)

President Donald J. Trump was inaugurated January 20, 2017. The next day the women of America responded with what has been reported as the largest single day demonstration recorded in United states history. (Chenowith, Pressman 2017) The march was born and flourished on the Facebook platform. The voice of the left took on a message of "resist" and still continues their message to the American public today through resist media platforms such as the #ResistTrumpTuesdays. They tout "We Have Just Begun To Fight. #RISEUP (People's Action 2017) The far left has lost touch with what it means to have respect for any kind of leadership and seems to just embrace anarchy as an answer. They seem to have no intention of coming together to solve issues. There is no positive message, just an agenda of resistance.

Wasting time on power seeking politics and rhetoric. With so much negativity towards the newly elected president, just who were those who voted for President Donald J. Trump in the 2016 election, the ones holding their breath, and celebrating victory? Big question here. After the stunning win in November 2016, many researchers scrambled to put together the facts that led to America's 45th presidential-elect.

There are different results, but the surveys seem to show that white votes were the underlying factor that tipped the presidential win. (Pew 2017) Is it fair to say that the white vote also tipped the presidential win for the previous POTUS, Obama? Who are the other conservative voters who expressed the will to elect a non-politician, white billionaire, previous Democrat into our nation's White House to govern the people and policies in this country where we have the privilege, not entitlement, of freedom? This and many more questions remain as we look forward and hope for the re-election of our current commander in chief, President Donald J. Trump.

There are a lot of exit polls out there to help the public understand the demographics of the voters who turned out in 2016, as well as those who didn't turn out to vote. Keep in mind that exit polls have results based on specific numbers of people polled. Also, as with any data or information we read; it is good to consider if the number polled shows an accurate representation of what we seek to understand. Be progressive and explore as there are many research sites to scour for more information. Some insights from both the Edison

Research group and the Pew Research Center for the outcome of the 2016 United States presidential election is, well, fascinating!

A Pew Research Center survey indicated that more Generation Xers voted than millennials in the 2016 election. This was surprising because more millennials voted in the previous election. Almost 36 percent of Generation Xers voted compared to approximately 34 percent of millennials. The baby boomers had the largest turnout with approximately forty-eight million voters, with Gen Z only coming in at about two million voters. It is predicted that millennials will outvote Gen Xers in the 2020 election. Per The Center on Generational Kinetics the age demographics for the different generations are as follows:

Gen Z, iGen, or Centennials: Born 1996 – TBD

Millennials or Gen Y: Born 1977 – 1995

Generation X: Born 1965 – 1976

Baby Boomers: Born 1946 – 1964

Traditionalists or Silent Generation: Born 1945 and before

Who are these Generation Xers, and will they turn out to vote again in 2020? Is there a group of individuals who did not turn out to vote in 2016? The higher percentage of women who came out to vote for Trump in 2016 were the baby boomers and the traditionalists. The lowest percentage of women who came out to vote for Trump in the 2016 election were from Generation Z. It is predicted that this age group of those born after 1996 will show up in higher numbers for the 2020 election.

In regards to race, 42 percent of white woman voted for Trump in 2016, while only six percent of African-American women voted for him. Approximately 19 percent of Hispanic women voted for Trump in 2016. The highest percentage of votes for Trump came from the white male and white female. Does this indicate that Trump is a racist? This is not at all evidential of racism, and he doesn't deserve to go through the pain of being called a racist. Among white voters, a higher percentage of those who voted for Trump were non-college graduates — the uneducated. Who are these uneducated? Possibly, the backbone and heartbeat of America.......the working middle class.

Chapter Two

The "Uneducated" in America

Educated is best defined as "having been educated," while uneducated is best defined as "having or showing little or no formal schooling, not educated." Intelligence is best defined as "the ability to acquire and apply knowledge and skills." (Merriam Webster) Based on the numbers from the Edison Research group (research involving 23,452 respondents), the breakdown of the education of voters at the polls in 2016 resembled the following:

High school or less	18%	(45% Clinton / 51% Trump)
Some College / Assoc.	32 %	(43% Clinton / 52% Trump)
College Graduate	32%	(49% Clinton / 45% Trump)
Post Graduate Study	18%	(58% Clinton / 37% Trump)

According to a United States Census survey, the number of degree holders in the United States has grown from 2000 to 2018. The numbers in millions are as follows:

	In 2000	In 2018
Bachelor's Degree	29.8	48.2
Master's Degree	10.4	21.0
Professional Degree	2.6	3.2
Doctorate Degree	2.0	4.5

An interesting fact to consider is the number of those who hold a professional or doctorate degree. Advanced degree holders in the United States are the minority. In fact, only approximately 13 percent of the total population of the United States holds a doctorate or professional degree. (America 2019) Think about that. *They* are the minority. *The*y are the "educated" elite liberals who are the first to tell others who are "uneducated" how to vote because, of course, the "uneducated" are unable to make their own decisions about what is best for their middle-class lives. I'm not buying it, and neither should you! Those elite liberals are also most likely in the highest income bracket of all the voters in the 2016 election.

The current population of the United States of America is approximately 329 million. As of July

2017, those eighteen years and over (of legal age to vote) number approximately 253 million. The states that hold the most voters include California, with approximately 30.5 million; Texas, with 20.9 million; Florida, with approximately 16.8 million; and New York, with approximately 15.7 million. These states total approximately 84 million votes. (https://www.census.gov/popclock/) That is approximately one third of the voting population in all of America! Thank God for our founding fathers who had the wisdom to establish the electoral college so that the president of the United States would not be elected by the most populous states in the Union. If that were the case, there would be no sense for the other forty-six states to vote.

Currently, the Democrats cannot accept the fact that their star guarantee election candidate, Hillary Clinton, was defeated by the governing of the electoral college system. Therefore, because she won the popular vote, Democrats are currently pushing for the removal of the electoral college system so that the United States president would only be elected by the popular vote. Had Hillary won, this discussion of the fairness of the electoral college would not be an issue. The liberal elite, not the majority of America's middle class who keep this nation's economy moving, want to keep power and control of the vote by patronizing any new immigrants or those they degrade into lower social classes.

In recent years, there has been a lot of talk about the patronizing of different minority groups by the Democratic Party. Patronizing can be defined as "an offensively condescending manner toward." (www.dictionary.com) It is inarguable that the United States has made great progress in the area of deep-rooted prejudices, with the understanding that there is always opportunity to keep moving forward. The liberal left will not move forward, however, and even goes as far as to demand the removal of statues that have been a part of the fabric of this nation's experiences and current existence. There is a force that continues to spread hate and erect barriers that detour the United States from progressing in thought and development as a country. Moving forward means understanding past history and, yes, actually growing from it. The United States is a freestanding nation and has only been in existence for 243 years! Think about that — 243 years. Many other countries have been around for thousands of years. Citizens born in the United States or who enter the nation legally should be proud and not ashamed of the hard work, perseverance, determination, and faith of the men and women who came before them. Think about their pain. Think about their hard work. Think about the lives lost.

Consider being grateful that we have a current POTUS, Donald J. Trump, who expresses his love and loyalty to the United States of America and to the American people. He is not about popularity and does not favor a certain group of people but concentrates on the American citizen. He leads from an understanding that we are all citizens, regardless of race, gender, or creed. Americans are blessed and should be proud to plan to vote for Trump in 2020.

The foundation of my career was working as a caseworker for the local Human Services, which is now called the Department of Job and Family Services. Being a caseworker at a young age educated me on the struggles of everyday life for families who were not able to work to provide for themselves. I had the opportunity during my career in Human Services to work in three demographically different communities. I was able to work in a small county with a growing surrounding housing area. Basically, taxes that would have gone to the city was being transitioned to county taxes for new schools and school districts. I learned quickly that in America, many families have different upbringings. Some families are not fortunate enough to have a working mother or father, and many households are run by one parent. People are actually living on government checks, medical care, and food stamps. Sitting across the desk from many different faces implanted in me a great deal of gratitude and appreciation for many small things in life. Some of the faces were "generational" faces. These generational faces were individuals who were raised with the belief that a government check would come at the first of the month, food stamps, medical care, and over-the-counter drugs would be provided, utility bills would be paid, and rent would be decreased or would be $0 a month. Studies have proved that generation after generation are living on the system. This was an expectation or entitlement for some of the families — a belief, a system. It was also a ceiling for little change or breakthrough. In some cases, the benefits became a mechanism that afforded the government the opportunity to tell people how to live. I resent the talent and intelligence that was wasted. The majority of these people were being patronized by political parties who made promises of securing that pitiful check and food stamps to feed un-fathered children at the first of the month.

Our country's Health & Human Services department is dictated and controlled by the executive branch. The "Welfare to Work" programs were going strong in the early 1990s. These programs started refocusing efforts and monies toward getting individuals back to work. Those on assistance were told they needed to get training or education or do some sort of community service to be entitled to the benefits they received. This was a welcome idea for those who really wanted to use the talents they had to become more self-sufficient, and that is just the term the government used to help these individuals develop a plan — a "self-sufficiency" plan. The idea would be for caseworkers on the front line to help individuals in the system identify their strengths and weaknesses, help design their own self-sufficiency contracts, and link them to resources in the community to help them meet a goal. Sounds awesome — right? Well, it was, to say the least, not taken very easily by those generational families who were taught that you could depend on government income for a way of life.

The self-sufficiency plans allowed for payment of daycare expenses, money to buy a first vehicle, and emergency funds available to help individuals and families meet their goals. Some of these goals included education programs. If you were enrolled in a college or university, that would basically meet your "sufficiency" requirement to receive your monthly benefits. College expenses were paid by governmental grants. Under this self-sufficiency initiative, timetables were set that explained to recipients that they would no longer receive benefits after a certain date — scary news for any individual or family! Many mothers learned for the very first time in their lives that they would have to leave their children at a daycare provider.

There were tears and frustration. Some individuals basically came in and said, "If I have to work for my benefits, then just close my account!" Other individuals became very angry and insisted that there was no way the government agency could expect them to follow through with a self-sufficiency plan.

Kudos to those individuals who recognized their intelligence and valued themselves enough to grow and take care of their families through self-sufficiency efforts. Every person who can see their own worth is a benefit and blessing to their families and to their communities. Kudos to all the American women who have always understood the pain of leaving children every morning at a daycare or with a trusted relative to go to work to provide enough income for their families to pay the bills, with little support from anyone. These women work to make it happen and see more in themselves than any government could ever see or understand.

The economy is another variable to salary expectations and possibilities for the middle class. If our country as a whole has a mindset of big government — big handouts, little personal expectations — then the vote in 2020 will turn out favoring the Democratic Party. If our country still believes in the value and understanding of how to create jobs, for more employment — and to trust that money will be used to better middle-class status

— then hopefully, the vote will be Republican. We need four more years — four more years of less patronizing and more thinking for ourselves. Four more years!

Common sense, hard work, persistence — this describes the middle class of America. The taxpayers are represented somewhere in the previous survey data. With all due respect, they represent an education of some sort as they are able to provide enough income to feed and clothe their families, and to pay their bills without the help of government assistance. They have the desire to get up, dress up, and show up every day at work to provide an income to their family. Faith to get through every single day. They show hard work and the power of faith and reliance on something bigger than themselves. They are parents modeling opportunity for spiritual growth and compassion — parents who believe in the American dream. Get up! Dress up! Show up to vote in the 2020 election for a president who also believes in these values.

Looking back at the 2016 election, could it be that Hillary Clinton did not understand the voice of the working, "uneducated," middle-class women (and men) in America? Or are the middle-class, working women of America happier and more satisfied than what the liberal left wants them to believe or be? Women do not need to liberal to be considered "equal" to men. Maybe they are conservative because they are aware of their own uniqueness as a woman. It could be said that conservatives are content with their identity and are accepting of their biological, emotional, spiritual, and psychological makeup. They like how they are designed, understand hard work, and don't have extreme expectations. They are housewives and businesswomen. They are factory workers and American soldiers. They are mothers and grandmothers. They are nurses and doctors. They are smart and loyal. The voters who turned out for the 2016 election are, in fact, "educated" about being Americans who have the freedom to vote.

Chapter Three

The Vote

W hat exactly is in a vote? It is our right as citizens of the United States of America to express freedom and individual free speech. For women and those of color, it is a freedom that was fought for and should be respected by all parties in our government. It is a voice that should not be silenced and a freedom that should not be dictated by any political party. No woman should be shamed by a political party because she doesn't agree with the morals, values, or ideals of that party. No women (or men) of any color or race that are United States citizens should experience this.

President Donald J. Trump gifted a patriotic celebration "Salute to America" on July 4, 2019, for the American public to celebrate. The American press and liberal lefts ridiculed the president, and most of the networks didn't air the celebration. There was rhetoric that the event would be shameful because there would be tanks and military flyovers. Boycotts were organized. The POTUS was referred to as a narcissist by the liberal press, and there was a lot of virtual meltdowns from the liberal left on social media. The event was wondrous. It was full of historic information that should make every American proud of the nation's will to survive. It is not a perfect history, but there is no country with a perfect history. The liberal left is determined to keep the people of the United States from feeling grateful and proud of a country that stands for freedom and liberty by taking extreme measures to silence any patriotism or conservatism. There is an important and strong history that helps Americans understand how far we have come as a country.

Less than one hundred years ago, our country adopted the 19th Amendment to the Constitution, which granted women the right to vote. Prior to this amendment, history carved out the first wave of the women's rights movement, or feminism, in the United States. There are four waves of the women's rights movement. The first wave is referred to as the *Political Movement*. This was a time in history around 1848 that we can refer to the first feminist movement. There were many efforts from different women prior to 1848; however, 1848 marks the rewrite of the Declaration of Independence that allowed women full citizenship. It was not unheard of for women to vote prior to this time; however, any woman voting was probably single and a landowner as any woman prior to the rewrite of the Declaration of Independence had to have an approval from a judge to vote. The right to vote came from the leaders of the Seneca Falls Convention, among others. These leaders included men and women who recognized women's right to vote and the need to include women in full citizenship status in the United States of America. In relation to these events, in 1849, Elizabeth Blackwell became the first woman in America to earn a medical degree.

Around this same time, there was an active voice from the abolitionists, who were those who urged that slavery be abolished. The importation of slaves was outlawed in America in 1808, but slavery was still legal in eleven southern states, where plantations depended on the work. By 1840, there were more than 150,000 members of abolitionist societies. One of the first women to help found the American Anti-Slavery Society was a white woman by the name of Lucretia Mott. She was a Quaker, as many abolitionists were Quakers of New England. Wendel Phillips, a New Englander, gave up his law practice to help join the abolitionist cause. Another by the name of William Garrison founded a newspaper, *The Liberator*, to speak specifically to the issue of abolishing slavery. The abolitionist cause gained fire and respect with black

Americans with the voice of Frederick Douglass, a freed slave, who joined the movement to help educate others about the need to abolish slavery.

An honorable abolitionist who was an avid supporter of anti-slavery laws, John Brown (1800-1859), was tried and convicted of treason for leading a raid on the federal arsenal at Harper's Ferry. He was hung in a public square in Virginia for promoting a slave revolt and murder. His four sons also fought with him for the freedom of slaves. At this time, the United States was on the brink of a civil war, and the Democratic Party was split. This is when Abraham Lincoln, a Republican, was elected into office in the month of March 1861.

From 1861-1865, the Civil War was fought over states' rights and slavery. The South- (eleven states) of the country wanted the freedom to make their own laws without answering to the federal government. The Southerners had large plantations and felt that their plantations would not survive without the manpower of the slaves as the slaves worked the plantations. The North wanted to abolish slavery. The cost of the Civil War was to the tune of 600,000 — 600,000 souls died for their beliefs. These were Americans fighting other Americans for their beliefs. This staggering amount of souls lost is almost as many as in all other American wars combined. These men, who preserved the Union, deserve some mention. More than twice as many soldiers died of diseases such as typhoid, malaria, and dysentery than were killed in battle. How sick — natural causes took their lives. The North lost approximately 364,000 soldiers, and the South lost approximately 258,000 soldiers — all for the home of the free and the brave. This is our history whether you like it or not. These are the facts whether you like them or not. Don't rewrite it. Be proud of the fight and the survival and be proud to be an American. Be brave, be free, and be healthy. Stop the hate between citizens of the United States. We'll get more into citizens in chapter five.

Black men were authorized to vote with the passage of the 15th Amendment. The women of society felt they should have also been included in the right to vote, and because black men had the right and privilege prior to them, there was a break off between races in the women's movement. Women like Carrie Chapman Catt began political campaigns and organized street picketing in front of the White House. She and her group of women faced numerous beatings, deplorable work conditions, and were arrested regularly. They did set the course for white women's right to vote. Another woman hero who fought for a woman's right to vote was Susan B. Anthony (1820-1906). She was a Quaker from Massachusetts who fought for the abolition of slavery and worked for the American

Anti-Slavery Society. She was also a leader of the National Woman Suffrage Association; however, she would not see the 19th Amendment passed as it occurred fourteen years after her death.

Because of the split and racial tensions between white and black women, black women were not included in the right to vote and would not be able to vote for the next forty years. Black Americans originated mostly from Ghana and Sierra Leone in West Africa and were brought to America in the 17th and 18th centuries. The word "negro" comes from the Spanish word for "black." During the early movements out of slavery, most black Americans wanted to be called African-Americans. They are United States citizens who deserve their place and should be very proud of their contributions and perseverance for freedom. They have overcome many obstacles, and the phrase "Black is beautiful" means just that. The character of men and women lies within, and the right for freedom has come a long way for those whose ancestors were slaves in this country. They have survived the hate and fear of the Ku Klux Klan, as well as many prejudices that have kept them in low-paying jobs and poor neighborhoods. The Ku Klux Klan was formed from Democratic support of soldiers from the defeated Confederate Army in 1866. The Klan attacked black people who were trying to use their right to vote. Through the years, the Klan has targeted Catholics, Jews, immigrants, and African-Americans.

Despite the hate groups, African-American citizens have distinguished themselves in government, business, the arts, and sports. They have every right as those of other American citizens. May there be positive movement forward. There are many excellent books written by black authors to enjoy, such as those written by Maya Angelou, who shared her experiences as a black woman in the United States, and Gwendolyn Brooks, who won the Pulitzer Prize for her poetry about her perspective of racial hatred and discrimination in the Chicago neighborhood where she lived. We are Americans.

Let's not forget, during the forty years that black women were unable to vote while white women could, the country was facing many other challenges, such as the Great Depression. This depression was a severe economic collapse that occurred after a stock market crash that disabled many workers in the country. The effects of this depression also affected other countries. From the period of 1929 forward, many farmers lost their farms due to extreme poverty. They had to lay off workers because of their inability to pay their debts. The Great Depression continued into 1933, which is believed to be the worst year suffered. Approximately twelve million Americans were unemployed and homeless, only able to stay alive through charity, begging, and working any job that was offered. There was a loss of more than 85,000 business. Imagine their state of mind — the despair, the tiredness, the looking for someone, anyone to fix the pain. Mothers, both black and white, were unable to feed their children. There was rationing of resources and food.

This Great Depression allowed for the strengthening of evil. In Germany, Adolf Hitler created the evil that would eventually lead to World War II. In 1939, the breakout of World War II gave the US economy an enormous boost to industry, bringing the Great Depression to an end. At this time, there was a burst of union organizing. Total union membership rose from about three million to ten million in 1941.

Women across America should know about the women heroes of the Second World War. In 1944, the women working in America rose from twelve million to twenty million. African-American, Asian, Hispanic, and white women worked side by side in factories building war planes and submarines for the military. Most of the women had husbands who had left for the war. These women learned to manage their families by sometimes living together so they could take turns watching their children and reporting to their factory jobs. They worked together to build airplanes, such as the B-17 and

B-24 bombers. Imagine the pride of these women when the finished products rolled off the assembly lines. Imagine the hard work, the feeling of really doing something for their country and husbands who were fighting for American lives while losing their own. The pride and accomplishment these women felt must have been remarkable. There was a popular song that hit the charts to give honor to these women. The women were called "Rosie the Riveters," and there was a national song produced for "Rosie." It was recorded by several artists. "Rosie" became a fictitious character to promote the need for women to become trained in industry jobs. (www.history.com)

These ideals also gave birth to the Women's Army Corps at the urging of then-First Lady, Eleanor Roosevelt. Congress instituted the Women's Army Corps in May 1942. The group began as the Women's Auxiliary Army Corps and was the first women's service branch in the Army. By 1945, another women's service group was formed — WAVES (Women Accepted for Voluntary Emergency Service). These women served in the Navy. The number of WACs was approximately 100,000, and the WAVES numbered approximately 6,000. There were 106,000 women serving for the protection and efforts of the United States of America!

After the WACs and WAVES came the WASPS (Women Airforce Service Pilots), numbering in at a little over 1000. These women had their pilot's licenses prior to entering the WASP initiative and flew over sixty million miles in order to free thousands of male pilots for active duty. The WASPS were responsible for ferrying the planes to the bases from the factories. They were only considered civil service employees, and thirty-eight lost their lives during the course of the war. These women were not recognized for full military status until 1977.

The recruitment for female workers was in full swing, and another patriotic group of women were termed "Wendy." Wendy represented "Winnie the Welder," better known as "Wendy the Welder," and they were part of the approximately 2,000 women who worked in the shipyards building ships. The homage of "Wendy" is represented by Jennifer Mann of *The Patriot Ledger*. Wow — great American women patriots in action!

She wore welding spats to protect her legs from the flames. Her helmet, with the name Flo etched across the front, shielded her eyes from the spraying sparks. With a heavy green welding jacket masking her 20-year-old figure, the long mane of auburn hair was the only clue that a young woman was building ships alongside the men at the Fore River shipyard in Quincy. (Mann 2019)

Yes — these women deserve respect and gratitude for their patriotic journeys. They were real women and represent the fight and perseverance of American women in the past. They were behind the scenes working, supporting, missing, loving, and staying loyal to our America. During these times of tremendous work effort, in 1944, the average weekly wage for female skilled workers was $31.21; the average for comparable males was $54.65.

Even though working side by side helped women of all ethnic backgrounds and creed to begin talking and understanding one another, the racial tensions between the white and black women of the country continued into the Second Wave of feminism in America, referred to as the *Social Movement.* This movement initialized itself through the Civil Rights Movement of the 1960s. Racism and sexism were alive and well in America after the Second World War. America was redefining its identity. During this time, women were regarded as less educated because most were not earning college degrees, and men were paid more than women. Women began to demand an end to sexual harassment in the workplace and adopted a slogan for the Second Wave, "The personal is political." The message to the government was for more women's rights. (Covington 2015)

In 1963, the Equal Pay Act was passed, stating that women should receive equal pay for equal work. Black women in America still had less of a political voice, though. The writings of authors like Alice Walker and Toni Morrison were pivotal in exposing the truth of the black female experience in America, giving a voice to those without one. *The Color Purple*, by Alice Walker, was a popular novel through which Americans learned page by page what it meant to be a black woman overlooked by the women's movement in America. Wheels of equality were turning. During the Social Movement, women were elected to Congress, and platforms were built for feminists to reach a broader audience. *Roe vs Wade* emerged in the efforts to allow women to take control over their own bodies. The Equal Credit Opportunity came into fruition, and Sandra Day O'Connor became the first woman on the Supreme Court.

The Third Wave of the feminist movement is called the *Individual Movement*. The Individual Movement was a movement that was more of a reaction to the prior movements, a separation of ideals and an opportunity for women to define their own feminism. This was not a cohesive wave. The 1991 hearings of Anita Hill against Clarence Thomas, a Supreme Court Justice nominee, regarding sexual harassment were followed closely by women across America. There were also demonstrations and ideals of women having their own voices and being able to use those voices against those who were homophobic or who committed violence against women. In 1994, the Violence Against Women Act was passed. Awareness of sexuality and the gaining of confidence in sexuality was a strong motivator of this wave.

The Fourth Wave of feminism emerged after 9/11; it could be argued that the Third Wave really never ended, but the Fourth Wave was more technologically savvy and realized its voice in the area of social media. It argued that women's bodies should not be used as objects of pleasure for others, and that women's bodies have been violated by the social media world, violated to incite feelings of shame to those women who could not live up to unrealistic expectations their male counterparts were being brainwashed to believe was the real woman's body. These Fourth Wave feminists are still sending the message that it is not okay to objectify women, and they are solidly against violence against women. With the recognition and passing of the 1994 Violence Against Women Act, it showed that we as a nation are against this type of treatment of women.

Some of the facts remain that women can still earn less than men; however, women have come a long way. They are designed to bear children, which does take away from some of the demands of working in some occupations; hence, the value of the output is not the same as a man. The women who support our current President Donald J. Trump support the man as a patriot leader. Currently, women make up about 20 percent of the Senate and a little less in the House of Representatives. The United States has a way to go if women want more representation, or should it be said that women have a way to go if they want more representation? The United States has never had a female vice president or president. This is true; however, is it sexism? Women currently make up 22 percent of CEOs of Fortune 500 companies. Women of America. Stay the course!

Today, we know there are many issues involving domestic violence. We must become more involved in our communities to aid those who suffer. The outcry of women in demonstrations across the country show that they all have stories, important ones. We all have a story. It's wonderful to see this. Be grateful we live in a country that allows us to voice our concerns and demonstrate peacefully. With this awesome right to demonstrate, however, some of the demonstrations are less than peaceful. The United States is becoming an entitled society where people want to cry injustice because they do not "feel" they are getting enough attention, enough of something. Really? Become "educated" in life and read the facts. Find gratitude and lose the dramatics. Embrace the history and appreciate the freedoms. What are the facts on how most of the women in this world live and are treated? We have men and women who came before us who fought and won many victories. What about the women in Saudi Arabi, Iran, and India? There are many, many more than just these three countries, but think about the injustice these women face every day. They do not have the freedom to speak to a male outside of their family for fear of being accused of adultery or prostitution and killed. The women in these countries endure honor killings and can be married off at as young as nine years old. Use the mind you were given and read the facts, facts that will bring you to gratitude. Let's show respect, American women, and move on!

As American women, we should feel ridiculous claiming we are oppressed while living in the United States. There is still work to be done in the area of equality, but we are moving forward. Let's do it respectfully. Every woman in the United States owns the history of America. It is ridiculous if the left thinks it owns oppression or if the right believes it is the only one working. We are in this together, and both sides need to own that we women were oppressed throughout history and that we have worked diligently and, hopefully, respectfully as women. Let's come together and teach our children and grandchildren the value of respect, not only for ourselves but for others. Build your local communities. Don't drag the heavy suitcase of hate around. Focus on some joy — seriously, drop the hate! Let's move forward in a courageous way, acknowledging and enjoying the freedoms of being American women. Run, don't walk to practice your freedom to vote for values in the 2020 election!

Chapter Four

Fear of "free" speech

Free speech — are you afraid, afraid to say you're voting for President Donald J. Trump in the 2020 election? A lot of social media feedback indicates that many women (and men) are afraid to admit they voted for Trump in the 2016 election, and many women are also afraid to show their support and say they are going to vote for him in the 2020 election, for fear of backlash from the left. Don't be silenced. The citizens of the United States are free people and should not be afraid to exercise their freedom of speech or freedom to cast a vote in 2020 for Donald J. Trump as our 46th POTUS. Are Americans afraid to voice support of the current president?

Remember all the outcry for resistance after the election of President Trump? To "resist" is best defined as follows: "to exert force in opposition." (www.dictionary.com) The entire theory of collusion being the reason President Trump was elected began with a statement released from Hillary Clinton after the election with the simple question of, "Why is Trump encouraging Russia to interfere in our election?" (Doran 2018) And there it is! It was the start to a wildfire that the poor loser lefts grabbed onto and fueled, just hoping to deteriorate any progress for our country to maintain its domestic and business affairs. It was a time-consuming, expensive venture to sidetrack the United States government and its citizens with the world watching. Collusion! So, the idea was born that Trump was conspiring with Putin — this became the perfect escape for Hillary Clinton. It was the perfect escape from the news of WikiLeaks and the perfect diversion from the real truth that Clinton was trying to hide while sabotaging the Republican Party in the meantime. The real story of power and collusion would be sidetracked.

There have been many publicized events of the backlash Americans face for wearing hats or clothing that read "Make America Great Again." It has been deemed a symbol of hate by the left, and participants proud of America, the land of the free, are considered hateful racists just for wearing any clothing that has MAGA (Make America Great Again) on it. It has become a crime to express loyalty and respect to our country, the United States of America. This country is a country that gives the freedom to dream. The people wearing the clothing and hats are most likely representatives of the Republican Party. Remember, the Republican Party was the party that was established based on ending slavery across America, the party that would not give up the fight to free slaves. Donald Trump's campaign voiced the desire to ignite patriotism and work on making America great! It was not about a desire to create inhumane living conditions. We have become a society of individuals who want everything to be about our feelings. Feelings are very complicated, and since we are not designed to be mind readers, we need to accept that the message "Make America Great Again" comes from a desire to help the economy and help us all become better citizens who complain less and do more for ourselves, our families, and our country. Can we believe this, or is America so weak-minded that citizens react defensively and create hate speech towards our own government, authority, and leadership?

"Eat this (expletive) pad, you c**k face!" was shouted at a pro-life activist in Ashland, Oregon in front of a Planned Parenthood at the March for Life in 2017. (Ertelt 2017) The pro-lifer was caught off guard as a twenty-one-year-old slapped a wet, bloody maxi pad in his mouth. What an ugly, hateful way to keep others from free speech and from voicing their concern over the ending of life and the idea that maybe there is a different approach or answer. This was a disgusting and vile act by a woman who demands "free speech." This behavior against the Right to Life advocate was not "free speech;" it was an assault and hate crime against another's free-speech efforts.

Attacks against Trump supporters increased in 2018. In New Jersey, an eighty-one-year-old was attacked by teenagers for wearing a MAGA hat. Two men in Maryland were charged with assault and robbery after attacking a man for wearing a MAGA hat. A man in New York wearing the hat was punched repeatedly in the head by unknown assailants. Another man living in New York who had recently bought a MAGA hat because he thought the president-elect was doing a good job was jumped by about fifteen teenagers and beaten brutally after he put on the hat. He was quoted as saying, "It's sad to get beat up for wearing this hat. This is America." Sad, indeed. (Gestaler 2019)

In the most recent mass shootings and after the mental anguish Americans experienced in August 2019, the liberal left rejected any and all statements from President Donald J. Trump. Trump was accused by a MSNBC news reporter that he was a president who seems to want these things to happen. Dan Rather was fast to tweet, begging journalists "to refrain from quoting the president's words from prepared speeches into headlines." (https://twitter.com/DanRather) No free speech for our President? What about the American citizens who wanted to hear from the president of the United States, the ones who have a differing opinion than those of the press? In another incident after the mass shootings, a mob showed up at Senate Majority Leader Mitch McConnell's with several threatening messages. One specific message voiced by a woman "Everybody needs to just show up..........and make him just regret his f***ing life period" (Ross 2019). Violently resist?

Democratic Congressman Joaquin Castro published the names of citizens who donated to President Trump's campaign in order to make them think twice about contributing. Anyone who expresses support for our current president is accused of being a white supremacist. If you support President Trump, you are reminded daily in the newspapers that you may be a victim of hate speech or actions of aggression from those who say they fight for free speech but will not tolerate any idea that is outside of their own. Trump supporters are called Nazis — really, Nazis?

Sarah Huckabee Sanders is one of only three women ever appointed to be the president's press secretary of the United States of America. You read that right — one of only three. She was appointed under our current POTUS, Donald J. Trump. Is that something a sexist would do? Sarah endured many public humiliations from the press during her time as press secretary. The only other two women who have held this position were Dee Dee Myers in 1993 and Dana Perino in 2007.

Sarah was brutally mocked by the liberal left and was basically bullied and tormented publicly with remarks from columnists, representatives, and the press about her weight. She was called a "whore" and a "harlot." She was referred to as "a slightly chunky soccer mom" and ridiculed about her accent, make-up, and clothes. (Kelly 2017) These outrageous remarks are a message to all women supporters of Trump and are not reflective of the grace and outstanding job our third female press secretary performed. The vile treatment of Sarah Huckabee Sanders dished up by the left liberals exists to plant fear in any conservative woman who voted for Trump in 2016 or who will think to vote for him in 2020. It is a stage for the Democratic Party to voice ridicule towards women who are Trump supporters. Sarah Huckabee Sanders gave her resignation in June 2019, after which she was quoted as saying it was the "honor of a lifetime" to serve in the Trump administration. "I've loved every minute — even the hard minutes." (Heightline 2019) America was graced by the minutes, hours, days, months, and years that she served.

Voting is a time to express free speech. It is time to think about voting, America. Exercise the right to vote, the right to have loyalty to the mission of President Donald J. Trump. Don't be ashamed of his mission to "Keep America Great!" There is no problem with this ideal, and other countries should embrace this as their ideal too. Vote to voice your approval, gratitude, and thanks to an American leader who is not interested in speaking to gain popularity but is interested in speaking to the hard-working, middle-class men and women of the United States. He is a president who is interested in meeting goals and getting to work for a better America. Don't be silenced by fear — just vote to keep America great through a leader who is not afraid to speak up and speak the truth. Trump knows how to stand up to liberal idealism. Be patriots. Be courageous.

Chapter Five

Immigration

E very person in America has a story — a story of their forefathers and the immigration path their family took to get to freedom. Whether your family roots landed with many of the English on the Mayflower or were part of the great Irish migration, we all have a unique story of our ancestors making it to the Free World. Immigration rules and regulations have changed through the years. Most American citizens have ancestors who came to this country legally and respectfully. They are grateful and understand the blessing we have to be a part of this great country. The paths carved were not easy and were ones that challenged the growth and development of individual character, and the sheer will to survive. Paths of great faith and the desire to be free — freedom from barbaric killings and to realize potential. Come along on the journey of one Macedonian family who fled the massacre of 40,00-50,000 men, women and children in the early 1900s. Everyone — farmers, carpenters, intellectual leaders, and anyone able-bodied — fought with all their hearts to stay alive and keep their family members safe. Experience their quest for freedom.

Sheika trembled as she pulled her daughter closer to her. She was cold, and numb; body, mind and soul.

She could smell her own fear. She closed her eyes, hoping that when she opened them she would be back home with her family, her husband. So much had changed and so fast! She wanted to keep her eyes closed forever. She did not want to see or deal with the horror and the pain that was now her life and the life of her daughter. Sheika pushed Mary aside and bolted from the cave. She heaved and heaved with pain. Her family was no more. Her home was no more. Her hopes, laughter, and dreams had turned into despair, tears, and a nightmare. "Give me strength! Give me strength, Great One!" she shouted as she fell to her knees. A sound she did not recognize poured out from her. She shook so hard she thought she might pass out. She grabbed on hard to the ground below her and could not bear the replay in her mind of the fire and screaming children....... the slaughter of her people. Minutes, or maybe more an hour, later, she heard the cry of Mary. "Get up, Sheika," she spoke out loud. "Get up!" Slowly, she rose and wiping her tears and blood -stained face, limped back to the cave. Taking a seat beside Mary. She comforted Mary and knew she could cry no more. She became a strong woman.

Nick, bloodied and shocked, continued his plan for escape. He couldn't look back, couldn't recount the horror of the seconds that had allotted him the mercy of survival. He could still vision the fight — the blood, the screams for help, the desire to turn back but knowing he had no choice but to move forward. He trusted and prayed Sheika would be safe with the others in the caves and hills of Greece. He had no choice but to believe. He needed to run — run far away, run for them all. His mind raced as his heart thudded with great persistence in his chest. He could feel and hear the blood flowing through his ears. He did not want to think or even be alive right now, but he had to stay alive for Sheika and his daughter. He had to. It was too risky to take his family with him, but he'd promised Sheika he would return to get her. *I must find freedom from the Turkish regime,* he thought. *I must move and create a life where my family can live and be free. There are no easy answers, no easy road ahead. My choice is bravery or death. I may never see Sheika again. I must make it to the New World. My God will take care of Sheika until I unite with her. My God is mighty. My faith is great.*

Nick tried to swallow but an apple-sized barrier prevented the reflex. *I must make it to the port. I must keep moving.* It had taken him several days to make it thus far. He was parched and weak from little food. His stench was unbearable; he smelled of blood and sweat. He was, after all, considered to be a "barbarian" by the Greeks — a Macedonian, a despicable barbarian. A man from the blood of Alexander the Great, who was tutored by Aristotle himself, was thought of nothing but a barbarian, not worthy of speaking his own language of Macedonian. He thought so hard about this that he was sure his heart would explode. He continued to vision the last minutes of his brothers, Alex and George being hung in the public square of his small home in the hills of Greece. The Turks were relentless and ruthless to his people. There was no room for him or his heritage. Blood and tears — body parts, and dead bodies of loved ones were all his people would remember of their existence. This thought pushed him further, further toward the port. He must find a way of life in the New World. He must have faith. He must not give up.

The many families hiding out in the mountains continued to grow. A small civilization was forming of women and children. They needed to keep faith that their husbands would return. The pain of missing their husbands was too great to bear.

They needed to have faith that moves mountains, faith *in* the mountains to which they called their home. It was a civilization born from fear and the desire to live, a civilization that could not succumb to fear. This civilization would starve without initiative, hard work, charity, and prayer. There were no amenities — just human stink, emotions, waste, and the desire to live. There was great faith in such a little existence.

Nick met kindness and support along the way to the port and was blessed to receive some comfort along his journey. He knew that he needed to make it to the New World to bring some sort of survival and sense to his and his family's lives. There was no other choice. After months of foot travel and travel by train, he made it to the port. He had thirty dollars left — thirty dollars. He saw many men without their families. His anger at himself for not getting out with Sheika and Mary before the attack turned him cold from the inside out.

Nick did not have a reservation for the ship voyage. He just needed to provide twenty-five dollars to have the opportunity to board. He was disappointed to learn that his wait to board the ship would be about three weeks. He waited, ate little, and slept where he could until it was his time to go through the boarding process. The morning before the 4:00 pm sail, he stood in line for hours, went through a medical examination, answered a questionnaire with at least thirty questions, was immunized and disinfected, and then stood in line again to anticipate boarding.

Nick smelled of disinfectant and stale body odor along with all the other passengers. Several passengers waiting in the long line puked from the putrid smell. *I want to live. I want to see my wife and children again* — these were the only thoughts Nick could think as he choked back tears. He blocked out all the noise and, in a surreal way, prepared himself to board the ship of opportunity. The ship headed to Ellis Island, America — the land of the free with great opportunity! He knew that many of his relatives and people of Macedonian descent were fleeing to Russia, Australia, and New Zealand. His arrow pointed to America.

"Sheika, Sheika, please help my baby! Sheika, please!" Sheika looked at the feverish and limp child that was brought to her. She gathered the child in her arms. The weakened cries of the baby were not a good sign. She asked for time from the mother. Sheika held the baby tight, rocking for hours and hours with the baby. She poured the medicinal oils that the farmers supplied her with on the baby. The food, the oils, the help all came from from answered prayer. Sheika had become the healer of the small mountain civilization. She needed healed but she would not stop giving of herself. She knew the baby she held was losing the fight to live. As she held her breath the baby breathed out it's last. Faith and her own daughter were the only vessels of hope in Sheika's crumbling life.

His brothers had been killed — killed without reason just because they were Macedonian! An anger and flush rose to Nick's cheeks. He thought of his beloved brothers and their love and service to the Macedonian people. His thoughts were interrupted as it was getting time to board. There were three types of passengers — first class, second class, and steerage. He was last to board in the steerage group. He could barely move from the overcrowding and looked around at what would be his prison for the next week to a month. It was unbearable as there were little to no accommodations. He could smell the puke left from previous passengers who had taken the voyage. He listened to the many stories of what was next to come. There would be more inspections and questions at Ellis Island. He learned that first-class and second-class passengers were given "courteous" inspections during the voyage and were transported to New York. Steerage passengers had to go through Ellis Island for continued inspections and questioning.

The movement of the ocean, the smell of the unbathed bodies, the lack of toilets available, and the overcrowding were so bad that many passengers felt the need to just jump overboard into the ocean to end their misery. The passengers bound for the promise of freedom would not give up hope. They would not forget their promises to the family members they left behind.

There she was; it was true! As the Statue of Liberty came into view, Nick felt an excitement, fear, and unbelief that he had never felt before. Eyes moved in every direction to catch sight of the advancing shoreline, and quietness fell across the ship. A deafening sound bore down and settled in each passenger's ear; the sounds of their own heartbeats thudded in anticipation of the New World.

Eventually, Sheika and her tribe were being-housed by good Samaritans in Edessa, Greece. The city was renamed to Edessa so it did not have a Macedonian name. Macedonians were unable to speak their native language and if any Macedonian spoke their mother tongue, they would be recognized and could be killed. Because Nick and Sheika had family in the Macedonian government, they were blessed with connections and with the concern and care of many. Sheika and her tribe would be okay until Nick returned to them. Her faith helped her through the moments, days, weeks, months, and years.

Seven years passed. After seven long years of working on the railroad and many evenings of exhaustive toil, Nick stood in line to welcome Sheika and Mary at the port.

It had been seven years of saving and working to establish a home for his family — seven years of his life spent creating a vision. Seven years of working exhaustedly in a free country, America! Nick was ready for his family to join him, but his legs shook beneath him as he spotted the ship that his wife and Mary were passengers on approaching.

The ship was a sight he had dreamed of each evening after he prayed and before he closed his eyes. Sheika, Sheika his sweet wife of long ago — how has she changed and Mary, would she recognize him? Nick was sweating profusely. Time was moving ever so slowly. So slowly, he thought he might choke on his own breathing.

Tears — no words, just raw emotion. Sheika's shrieks of joy pierced the air. She could not let go and could not think of looking Nick in the eyes. She just needed to hold on and never let go. Visions spiraled, and all noise was in the distance. Mary looked on wiping her tears of pain. She felt like a stranger but felt at home in her fathers embrace. They were a family. Her father was weathered but he was alive. He was really alive!

This immigrant family settled in a small town in Ohio. Nick had prepared a way of life for his family. He owned a small grocery store, and through his hard work out in the western states, he had saved enough money to send for his family. His family would have freedoms that they never could have imagined. They had the freedom to speak their own language and not fear of death because of it. Nick and Sheika never learned English, but their children could speak both Macedonian and English. Their children would live with a mother and father who knew of and understood a previous world where no freedom existed. Nick and Sheika's children had a foundation of great faith and were citizens of gratitude. Their children practiced loyalty to a country by serving in the Air Force and Army. They cherished the privilege of freedom and raised their children to have respect for a country that blankets their citizens with the privilege of living free! The American flag was a precious and glorious symbol of the birth of such a great country - America!.

The immigration process to become an American citizen has rules and laws. Currently, America has a population of approximately 329 million. Back in the early 1900s, the American population grew to approximately 106 million. To be considered a citizen means that you are a full member of a country. A citizen has certain duties and privileges. The right to vote begins at the age of eighteen. There is also a right to protection when living abroad if one is a United States citizen.

People not born in the United States have the right to become naturalized citizens through a legal process. The naturalized citizen swears allegiance to the United States of America and gives up loyalty to his/her country of birth. Naturalized citizens can vote but cannot become vice president or president. Since 9/11, there are many reasons the United States must be cognizant of those who come into our country and become citizens of this great land. We need government leadership that loves and protects America and the Constitution and is not ashamed of our existence as a freestanding nation.

It is inarguable that in every country there is a need for immigration. There is a basic economic need for hard-working individuals to come to a country, bringing with them the desire to work. This builds the labor force, and promotes GDP. Also, the addition of human capital to a country is always very important for innovation and the promotion of technological change. This America, land of the free, has flourished considerably with the great minds of diversity at work!

Another great reason for immigration is for the value of entrepreneurship — oh, that word, *entrepreneurship*. It represents the workers and builders who bring motion to the economy, the ones who create jobs for others and have that positive attitude! The United States of America is indeed in need of more entrepreneurs.

With these thoughts of great reasons to accept immigrants from other countries, why has our president been so criticized for his administration's handling of the border crisis? Again, it's a ploy, an untrue message from the press that we have a heartless leader. The POTUS administration's actions demonstrates a voice of reason and humanity. The law to separate children from the parents of those who enter the United States illegally was passed by the Clinton administration in 1996. President Obama, faced with questions about separating children from illegal immigrants during his presidency, explained that he was just implementing the rule that Clinton passed for two terms. Trump is just doing the same thing. He is also not afraid to address the drugs and crime that enter our country, and his administration is initiating action to put a stop to it. The left is still in a state of shock about losing the election and they start "politicking" because the liberals need these immigrants here *now*, with haste! The left wants to organize numbers to enter the country now. Why? The vote — they need to patronize for the vote. The vote doesn't come from United States citizens laying in trash cans at abortion clinics. The voice of each of these citizens is silenced. There is no outcry for these lives because the aborted lives disposed of have no voice to vote.

The United States is so rich and blessed with different ethnic groups that we are sometimes referred to as a "melting pot." The United States can boast a beautiful heart of acceptance of all ethnic groups and people who choose to become American citizens. America is the land of the free, where different ethnic groups are welcome to hold festivals and ceremonies that keep their unique heritages alive. Ethnic groups are alive in all areas of American society, and through the years, there has been a beautiful collection of individuals seeking religious freedom and those who work on building better lives for themselves. So why all the hate speech of discrimination from the left? The hate speech will brainwash and get them the vote.

There has been suffering along the way. African Americans were forced to come to this country as slaves, and Native Americans, Indians, Eskimos, and Aleuts were present on the land we call the United States long before Europeans. The beautiful land of America deserves to be called a "nation under God" and identifies itself with laws and rules to follow for the benefit of current citizens.

The current crisis at our Mexican border is a just that — a crisis. It is a crisis for our government officials, a crisis for the men and women who protect our border daily, and a terrible crisis for the immigrant children. The march of immigrants vowing to cross our borders in 2017 has not been a peaceful or legal trek to citizenship. The caravan of immigrants sent authoritative messages to our United States government that they would be crossing over into America whether or not we were ready and able to provide for their care. This is not the right way to become a citizen of any country. This is criminal mentality. Should our country tolerate anarchy? No. Vote for common sense. Vote for an organized structure towards legal immigration and implore those to come who hold an agenda to keep America great!

"Today, American people are apt to think too small. Please remember the good old days......Now is the day to rebuild the United States......"Think Big" and restart the movement toward "Greater America." (Okawa)

Chapter Six

Sanctity of Life

A gunman opened fire and murdered more than twenty living souls and injured over two dozen others in an El Paso, Texas shopping complex in August 2019. Another gunman, this time in Dayton, Ohio, suited up in full armor and enacted another mass shooting at a historic venue outside a bar, killing nine and injuring over twenty, less than twenty-four hours after the shooting in El Paso. What a disregard for the sanctity of life.

The response from President Trump was, "In one voice, our nation must condemn racism, bigotry, and white supremacy. These sinister ideologies must be defeated. Hate has no place in America. Hatred warps the mind, ravages the heart and devours the soul…We must seek real bipartisan manner – that will truly make America safer and better for all."

The response from most liberals in the United States was a response of hate — hate and a stubbornness against uniting for the benefit of the sanctity of life. The POTUS visited both cities to show his respect to the communities and to the victims' families with a promise of action on better gun control. This action of better gun control laws obviously wasn't taken care of during previous administrations.

The liberal left gets excited about the opportunity to try and abolish the American citizens right to bear arms. They attack the POTUS in a time of very deep pain. A pain -the loss of American citizens. The pain of realizing somewhere the individuals who carried out the plan to kill had no respect. No respect for themselves, their communities; their freedoms or life itself. In light of the politicking, the former Democratic Party Head, Donna Brazile brought some common sense to the American people by saying that the POSTUS did not bear the responsibility of the actions of the two shooters in Texas and Ohio and she was quoted by the New York post of saying the following:

"This conversation about race and racism, domestic terrorism, white supremacy, white nationalism, it is that I am profoundly saddened as an American. To point fingers, and to play this so-called blame game." (New York Post)

Without question, life is sacred, fragile, and a gift from our Creator. Abortion is a choice to kill or not to kill. A baby's heart begins to beat in the third week of development. The miracle of eyes is visible during the eighth week of pregnancy. The baby can feel pain at twenty weeks — pain of being sucked out of the womb and, in some cases, the pain of being dismembered. This is murder. Why aren't people outraged? Some statistics report that only .5 percent of abortions are the result of a rape incident — yes, .5 percent. African-Americans suffer from an "anti-life" campaign through abortion procedures as the process (abortion) is the number one killer of African-Americans. (Future Female Leaders 2018) Where's the outrage?

The evil of murdering a child is enough, but some abortion clinic doctors have actually been recorded discussing the abortion process with attitudes of humor. In one example, it was discussed how "the fetus is a very tough object" and how difficult a baby is to take apart.

One doctor was recorded joking, "An eyeball just fell down into my lap, and that is gross!" (Dreher 2017) Illinois, a state with gun control, has just passed an abortion bill that would allow abortion through the ninth month of pregnancy and even during the birth of the child. The Democratic leader, Governor J.B. Pritzker, signed the law into effect in June 2019. There is no voice for the butchered child who endures this practice of murder — pure evil. (Warren 2019)

Studies show that American women who have abortions suffer a 154 percent higher probability of suicide than women who carry their babies to full term. (Future Female Leaders) This study included 200,000 participants. Over half of documented abortions are completed on women under the age of twenty-five, and some studies indicate that there is a higher probability of child abuse committed by mothers who have previously had abortions. If a woman has suffered multiple abortions, there is a likelihood she may become dependent on public assistance. Understanding the facts of abortion is traumatic — imagine the pain and suffering of the women who have gone through this process?

There is the argument that if God is so great then there is always forgiveness. That is the easy part to understand — yes, the God of the Bible is able to forgive. His grace and love are bigger than the evil in this world times millions; however, the pain is in the minds and hearts of those who suffer the loss, and it is the lack of self-forgiveness that can often lead to physical, mental, spiritual, and psychological pain of women who are victims of abortion. Some family members vehemently reject letting their loved ones have an ultrasound prior to their decision to abort. The outrage comes from the point that if a young pregnant mother sees the living child in her womb, she may decide to go ahead and carry the baby to full term. We are becoming a society that doesn't have time to be bothered with taking responsibility fo behaviors and actions. A society that lacks the value of the preciousness of life itself.

The sweet protection of the womb — the Bible mentions the womb over sixty times. The sweet beginning of a heartbeat, the flutter of life, is God's creation. There have been over sixty million documented abortions by American citizens from 1973-2015. (LifeNews.com) God help the country of America. These were United States citizens who were aborted. These numbers come from the Guttmacher Institute; whose surveys come directly from abortion clinics. These aborted lives are thrown in trash cans, and some are harvested for their organs.

The DNA of each of these human beings is distinct to that individual -wow, what an awesome Creator! The liberals scream for the right to be able to end the lives of the babies they carry within. These babies' voices aren't important to most politicians, as these voices can't vote.

These babies' voices are important to Donald J. Trump – he remains steadfast in his understanding and belief in the sanctity of life. He understands that responsible American citizens should have the right to bear arms and that more is needed to protect the innocent lives in America. He has initiated the much-needed discussions and importance of recognizing the "red" flags that do not warrant gun sales to certain individuals. We need to trust that some change will finally come to fruition with a man who keeps his promises; who understands we have a right to protect but not a right to murder.

Understand the value of the vote, the vote for unheard voices. Vote to cease the pain and suffering in abortion clinics across the United States of America. Vote to end the failure of democratic led gun control states that boast the highest percentage of murders in the United States. Their gun control rhetoric is not the answer. Vote for values and respect to be instilled in the American people. Respect of self, respect for family; respect for community; respect for our police officers and first responders; respect for the right for citizens to bear arms; the respect for individuals to take responsibility for their own actions or inactions. Go to the polls in 2020 and let your red, beating heart decide on issues such as the evil disregard for the creation of life.

Chapter Seven

The Women BESIDE Trump

Melania Trump

Melania Trump – the First Lady of the United States. The FLOTUS, Melania, emulates class, beauty and kindness, the face and voice of an immigrant who was born a Slovenian. She moved to the United States in 2006 as a model and very proudly became a United States citizen ten years afterwards. Melania is only the second First Lady born outside of the United States, and she is currently the only First Lady who has become a naturalized citizen. She was appointed as a goodwill ambassador by the American Red Cross in 2015 and served for four years. Melania also served as honorary chairwoman for the Boys' Club of New York for five years, and she was named Woman of the Year in 2006 by the Police Athletic League. She has a passion for children and has participated in

National Child Abuse Prevention month. Melania launched her own jewelry company in 2010, and in that same year, she raised approximately $1.7 million for the American Heart Association. What a woman! Hers is a story of an immigrant from humble beginnings who moved to America to work hard and become a citizen legally.

Melania is an elegant First Lady who concentrates her duties on children. She emphasizes how the child should be protected, taught, and empowered. She has traveled the world and visited schools and hospitals. She also has a passion for raising awareness of the destruction caused by opioid abuse. She has a passion that she identifies as three pillars — recognizing the social and emotional health of children, social media availability tochildren and how it affects them, and the opioid epidemic. She has rolled out her "Be Best" initiative and will continue working and making waves in these very important issues in thecountry. While many politicians are politicking to earn their "power" positions, our First Lady is quietly going to the dark corners with those hurt and filled with despair. She works to make a difference in the lives of American citizens. She is a woman who can relate to Generation Xers.

Kellyanne Conway

The warrior woman behind Trump's campaign efforts is Kellyanne Conway, the first woman ever to run a successful presidential campaign. Wow! Women of America should be cheering this gal on! She is hardworking and unbending. She has business intelligence and a political science degree. In 1995, Kellyanne founded her own firm called The Polling Company.

While running the 2016 campaign, she must have related to middle-class women voters. Did they see themselves in her, working tirelessly, not giving up? She doesn't back down and speaks boldly and candidly.

Kellyanne Conway defends the current POTUS with accuracy, truth, and passion. President Donald J. Trump believed in Kellyanne's character and integrity to run his campaign as professionally as she did. He knew her potential and understood the value of her work.

Again, she was the first woman to run a successful presidential campaign in the United States — our president is not a sexist. He believes in capitalism and the self-actualization of women and men. Kellyanne Conway is the advisor of the 45th president of the United States and is a representation of the hardworking Generation Xers.

Ivanka Trump

Beautiful Ivanka Trump is currently serving as advisor to the President of the United States Donald J. Trump. Ivanka is also Donald's Trump's daughter. She was born in 1981 and represents the millennials' mindset. Ivanka is a successful fashion model and author. She has proved herself to be an exceptional businesswoman and is the executive vice president of development and acquisitions at the Trump Organization. Ivanka holds a bachelor's degree in economics and is married to Jared Kushner. Jared is of Jewish descent, and he and Ivanka have held on to their relationship for over a decade now. Jared serves as senior advisor to President Trump.

Ivanka is currently experiencing decline in her product lines from all the anti-Trump rhetoric; however, she has the grace and know-how to rise above the criticisms. She has her own line of clothing, shoes, and accessories. Entrepreneurship, beauty, and a business mindset — don't hate her because she is both intelligent and beautiful.

Ivanka serves as Co-chair of the national council of the American Worker, which was established by President Trump in 2018. Since inception, the program has had 85,000 students sign up nationwide. The roll out of the program was concentrated with Google and the White House is currently working on a pledge to retrain workers for work at over 350 companies including not only Google but the following: American Airlines, AT&T and Toyota. Exciting indeed! There will be available over 14 million training opportunities in the next five years!

Ivanka's initiative to provide support to women of other countries is monumental. The impact of creating avenues of entrepreneurship and help women develop skills in their own country of residence strengthens their existence and creates opportunities for growth. She understands that the economic development will need to have many checks and balances. Imagine that - "rigorous program" of ensuring that monies are being spent responsibly for the development of women. She plans to equip the women of Brazil, Chile, Columbia, Mexico, Peru, Indonesia and Africa with skills that will enable them to flourish on their own. These initiatives are what American leaders do to help other countries build their own value. Go Ivanka!

Betsy DeVos

Nominated by President Donald J. Trump, Betsy DeVos serves as the eleventh U.S. secretary of education. She formed her passion to help underserved children gain access to a quality education after serving as a school mentor for at-risk students in Grand Rapids, Michigan. Betsy's mother was a teacher and educator, and Betsy has over three decades of experience as an advocate for children and a voice for their parents. DeVos has served on many national boards, including the Kennedy Center for Performing Arts, Kids Hope USA, ArtPrize, Mars Hill Bible Church, and the Kendall College of Art and Design. Prior to her appointment, she was serving as chairman of the Windquest Group. In her quest for empowering parents, Betsy is advocating to restore control of education to the states and localities, giving parents the power to choose schools that are best suited for their children. Betsy has worked to create new educational choices for students in over twenty-five states and the District of Columbia in her leadership efforts in the area of improving education.

And let's not forget the renowned five Republican changemakers — Kennedy Copeland, who is willing to stand up to the left to voice her support for values; Candace Owens, who is the new voice for black American conservatives; Dana Loesch, who speaks candidly about the right to bear arms and emulates patriotic spirit; Tomi Lahren, who takes the liberal left ideals straight on; and Elisha Krauss, who through *The Daily Wire* leads daily talking points against the left's agenda. Diamond and Silk never disappoints with their all-out honesty and they are currently putting their lives on hold for their "Chit Chat Live Tour" to continue their talk on why they plan to vote red.

These women will all be voting "red" in the next presidential election. They are voting for patriotism and values. How many more women will vote red to support the patriotism and common-sense values Americans need to move forward without all the anarchy, hate, and rhetoric of the extreme left?

Chapter Eight

2020 Election

What is the electoral college? It is the group of individuals who elect the president and vice president of our United States of America, based on whichever candidates receive the most votes in their states. Every state has at least one representative. Each state has two senators, and those senators are elected to serve for a term of six years. The House of Representatives has representatives based on the population of each state, which means that the states with the largest populations, like California and New York, can have as many as several dozen representatives. There are always 435 representatives. These 100 senators and 435 representatives will decide who the next president of the United States will be in 2020. The president of the United States must be a natural-born citizen of at least thirty-five years of age and have been a resident of the United States of America for at least fourteen years. This president will have executive power over our nation and will be responsible for developing national and foreign policies, preparing budgets, and appointing federal officials. In addition, the president will be responsible to enforce federal laws, be the chief executive officer of the government, and be the commander in chief of the armed forces — the armed forces being the Air Force, Army, Marines, Navy and Coast Guard.

Donald J. Trump keeps his promises. He accomplishes what he sets out to do, and many believe that his first 500 days of office have been the best first 500 days of any presidency since George Washington! Since his inauguration on January 20, 2017, he has been working tirelessly to do what he says and say what he does! A reminder of his speech after election 2018:

> "As I've said from the beginning, ours was not a campaign, but rather an incredible and great movement made up of millions of hard-working men and women, who love their country and want a better, brighter future for themselves and for their families. It's a movement comprised of Americans from all races, religions, backgrounds and beliefs who want and expect our government to serve the people - and serve the people it will."

"We're going to get to work immediately for the American people. And we're going to be doing a job that hopefully you will be so proud of your president. You'll be so proud. Again, it's my honour. It was an amazing evening. It's been an amazing two-year period. And I love this country. Thank you. Thank you very much." (Sky News)

And get to work he did!

Economy

There is no doubt on either side, Democratic or Republican, that the activity of the stock market has enjoyed exceptional highs since the Trump election in 2016. As of August 2019, the market was up by more than a third of what it had been prior to January 2016. The Dow has been breaking history records and came in at over 26,000 points, an all-time high in the entire history of the Dow Exchange! This kind of activity explodes 401k retirement accounts. The gross domestic product or GDP hit the highest ever recorded in American history at the end of the first quarter of 2018! (Picardo 2019) GDP is important in a global sense. It can be viewed as the monetary "health" of a nation. The gross domestic product considers a country's consumer spending, business spending, government spending, the value of imports, and the value of exports.

The new tax law passed will help millions of Americans see fewer federal taxes taken from their paychecks, and many companies' taxes have decreased. This results in more bonuses paid directly to employees and middle-class families enjoying more expendable income for their families. This expendable income strengthens communities and creates more employment.

Approximately three million jobs have been created since President Trump's election. Since his election, the administration has seen over nine times more Americans working in the United States history. Manufacturing and construction jobs have increased. In addition, the number of working American exceeds any numbers reported since 2001. (Picardo 2019)

Foreign Policy

President Trump prioritized following through with discussions of the denuclearization of Korea and was successful in securing the return of seventeen Americans who were being held overseas. During his trip to China, he became the first president to dine in the Forbidden City since the founding of modern China, and during his trip to Asia, he negotiated over $300 billion in deals for the United States. During his first trip abroad, in addition to meeting fifty leaders of Muslim countries, he also met the pope. (Holt 2017) On that trip, the POTUS set the stage and addressed the need to remove radicals who prove to be a danger to any governing society. Most impressively, ISIS has been reduced to a mere less than 1,000 in number, when the previous administration had said the group would be around for at least a generation. One of his campaign promises was to the state of Israel. Jerusalem has been declared the capital of Israel, and the United States Embassy is now located in Jerusalem. This declaration is vital to the fundamental security of Jerusalem.

US Policy

President Trump just recently signed the "Promoting Free Speech and Religious Liberty" Executive Order. This POTUS is leading the global mindset of giving back religious freedoms. Trump also addressed the United Nations with a plea to end the decades long violence against Christians and other religious groups across the globe. He is the first American President to bring "religious" freedoms to the podium of the United Nations.

In the first 100 days of his presidency, Donald J. Trump signed over 90 executive orders! Some of the actions include the following:

Instituting travel bans for individuals from a select number of countries embroiled in terrorist atrocities.

Protecting law enforcement.

Mandating for every new regulation to eliminate two.

Defeating ISIS.

Rebuilding the military.

Building the border wall.

Cutting funding for sanctuary cities.

Approving the Keystone and Dakota pipelines.

Reducing regulations on manufacturing.

Placing a hiring freeze on federal employees.

Exiting the US from the TPP.

In addition to these executive orders, President Trump has been responsible for confirming more circuit court judges than any other United States president in his first year.

Somehow, this amazing POTUS continues to make time to visit the American people to let them know he is still in touch with them, that he hasn't forgot about them. He is on track to visit as many states as he can and works tirelessly. Through his completion of the "Thank You Tour" of post-inaugural rallies, midterm rallies, and 2020 rallies to date, he continues to inspire and validate his ability to lead and focus on meeting the goals of the American people.

Our current POTUS, Donald J. Trump, is not ashamed to proclaim his love for God and to speak of the faith he needs to lead the United States of America. He surrounds himself with intelligent people who he knows can get goals met. He is unabashedly a pro-life advocate. Trump is not worried about being popular. He is worried about working tirelessly every day to fulfill his promises and leadership to the American citizen. He is not a perfect human being — is there such a thing? He has proven his support of helping others meet their own self-actualization, regardless of race, creed, or sex. He is driven towards meeting goals and wants to respect and voice the ideals of the American citizen. He works diligently on speaking directly to and informing the American citizens about his daily and weekly schedule. He is authentic and a leader. Understand and appreciate that not everyone has it in their DNA to be leaders. How many potential American leaders have been aborted? Stay on the path to some common sense and a respect for our beloved United States of America. Our current President believes "No dream is too big; no challenge is too great". (Sky News) Keep the dream alive, and keep America great by voting RED in the 2020 election!

Women Vote RED!

Get involved by visiting

https://gop.com/get-involved/volunteer/
Consider sending a copy of this book to a friend!
Visit our Facebook Website @ Women Vote Red
for the discussion.

About the Author

R uth Snow is a Midwesterner, who lives in the "Buckeye" state. She works as an adjunct professor and has previous experience working as a case-worker with the Department of Job and Family Services under policy changes from the Bush and Clinton Administration. She received her undergraduate and MBA as a working mother of two. Ruth has been involved with teaching inter-national students at the collegiate level and ESL to younger students. She is passionate about human services and education and lives with her husband of seventeen years.

References

American Counts Staff, "About 13.1 Percent Have a Master's, Professional Degree or Doctorate", February 21, 2019 https://www.census.gov/library/stories/2019/02/number-of-people-with-masters-and-phd-degrees-double-since-2000.html

Anderson, Stuart, "3 Reasons Why Immigrants Are Key To Economic Growth", Forbes, October 2, 2016 https://www.forbes.com/sites/stuartanderson/2016/10/02/3-reasons-why-immigrants-key-to-economic-growth/#7fa21afe7dab

Bearingarms.com, retrieved 8/6/2019 https://bearingarms.com/tom-k/2019/08/06/statement-el-paso-dayton-shootings/

Berenson, Tessa, "Donald Trump Wins The 2016 Election" November 2016 Time https://time.com/4563685/donald-trump-wins/

Covington, Elle, "Women's Equality Day, A Very Brief Timeline Of Feminist History In America, Bustle, August 26, 2015, https://www.bustle.com/

articles/106524-on-womens-equality-day-a-very-brief-timeline-of-feminist-history-in-america

Chastin, Mary, "Oppression of women in America?", Legal Insurrection, January 23, 2017, https://legalinsurrection.com/2017/01/oppression-of-women-in-america/

Chenoweth, Erica, Pressman "This Is What We Learned By Counting The Women's Marches, Washington Post, 2017 https://www.washingtonpost.com/news/monkey-cage/wp/2017/02/07/this-is-what-we-learned-by-counting-the-womens-marches/

CHIT CHAT LIVE TOUR https://www.diamondandsilkinc.com/chit-chat-tour/

Council of Research Into South-Eastern Europe, "The Balkan Wars and the Partition of Macedonia", retrieved 8/1/19, http://www.historyofmacedonia.org/PartitionedMacedonia/BalkanWars.html

Dan Rather (@Dan Rather) https://twitter.com/DanRather

DemocraticUnderground.com https://www.democraticunderground.com/100212240981

Dictionary by Merriam Webster, http://www.merriam-webster.com/dictionary

Dictionary.com, https://www.dictionary.com/browse/patronize

Doran, Michael, "The Real Collusion Story", National Review, March 13, 2018 https://www.national review.com/2018/03/russia-collusion-real-story-hillary-clinton-dnc-fbi-media/

Dreher, Rod, "An Eyeball Just Fell Into My Lap", The American Conservative, May 25, 2017, https://www.theamericanconservative.com/dreher/eyeball-fell-into-my-lap-abortion/

Encyclopedia Britannica, https://www.britannica.com/topic/electoral-college

Ertelt, Steven, "Women Arrested After Shoving Her Bloody Pad Into Pro-Life Advocate's Mouth,

February 6, 2017, https://www.lifenews.com/2017/02/06/woman-arrested-after-shoving-her-bloody-pad-into-pro-life-advocates-mouth/

Fink, Jack, Google CEO, Sundar Pichai, Ivanka Trump To Announce Expanded Worker Training Program in Dallas, February 6, 2017, https://www.lifenews. com/2017/02/06/woman-arrested-after-shovingher-bloody-pad-into-pro-life-advocates-mouth/

Future Female Leaders https://futurefemaleleader.com/20-facts-will-make-pro-life/

Holt, Jim, "Complete List Of Trumps Accomplishments In The First 100 Days" 2017 Gateway Pundit thegatewaypundit.com https://www.thegatewaypundit.com/2017/04/

draft-complete-list-of-president-trumps-accomplishments-in-his-first-100-days/

Glum, Julia, "The Moment the Liberals Knew Trump Won: 24 Horrified Quotes, Pictures, And Tweets That Capture Election 2016" 11/8/17 https://www.newsweek.com/trump-election-anniversary-liberal-reactions-clinton-loss-704777

Gregg, Christina, "How many states did Trump win? A state-by-state look back at the 2016 presidential election," Aol. July 5, 2017 https://www.aol.com/article/news/2017/07/05/how-many-states-did-trump-win-state-by-state-look-back-2016-presidential-election/23017643/

Gstalter, Morgan, "New York man says he was attached by group of teens for wearing MAGA hat", The Hill, August 1, 2019 https://thehill.com/blogs/blog-briefing-room/news/455795-new-york-man-says-he-was-attacked-by-group-of-teens-for-wearing

Green, Emma, "Jerusalem Is Not the Explosive Device – It's the Detonator" December 5, 2017 https://www.theatlantic.com/international/archive/2017/12/jerusalem-embassy-capital-trump/547592/

Huange, Jon, Samuel Jacoby, Michael Strickland, K.K. Rebecca Lai, "Election 2016: Exit Polls", New York Times, November 8, 2016, https://www.nytimes.com/interactive/2016/11/08/us/politics/election-exit-polls.html

References

History.com, "Rosie the Riveter", Updated June 6, 2019 – Original April 23, 2010 https://www.history.com/topics/world-war-ii/rosie-the-riveter

Heightline, "Who is Sarah Huckabee Sanders' Husband? Her Family and Full Biography, https://heightline.com/sarah-huckabee-sanders-full-biography/

Kelly, Julie, "The Double Standard for Trump Spokeswoman, Sarah Sanders", National Review, December 12, 2017, https://www.nationalreview.com/2017/12/sarah-huckabee-sanders-chelsea-handler-sexist-double-standard/

LifeNews.com January 2018 retrieved 8/1/19 https://www.lifenews.com/2018/01/18/60069971-abortions-in-america-since-roe-v-wade-in-1973/

Linge, Mary Kay "Former Democratic Party Leader Donna Brazile Doesn't Blame Trump For Shootings", New York Post, August 10, 2019. https://nypost.com/2019/08/10/former-democratic-party-leader-donna-brazile-doesnt-blame-trump-for-shootings/

OhRanger.com, "Ellis Island National Monument, The Immigrant Journey", http://www.ohranger.com/ellis-island/immigration-journey

Mann, Jennifer, "Wendy the Welder: Former female shipbuilder recalls war days ", The Patriot Ledger, May 6, 2019 https://www.patriotledger.com/x1076903616/-WINNIE-THE-WELDER-Former-female-shipbuilder-recalls-war-days

Neatopoints.com, "Winnie the Welder", January 20, 2013, https://www.neatorama.com/2013/01/20/Winnie-the-Welder/

News by Clarence, "Who Really Is Kellyanne Conway? Find Out the Professional Details of Counselor to the President, ArticleBio, February 13, 2017, https://articlebio.com/who-really-is-kellyanne-conway-find-out-the-professional-details-of-counselor-to-the-president

People's Action, 2017 #ResistTrumpTuesdays https://peoplesaction.org/resist-trump-tuesdays/

Pew Research Center, "2016 General Election Preferences Among Men and Women". July 28, 2016 https://www.pewresearch.org/fact-tank/2016/07/28/a-closer-look-at-the-gender-gap-in-presidential-voting/ft_16-7-29-gender2/

Picardo, Elvis, "The Importance of the GDP", Investopedia, May 18, 2019, https://www.investopedia.com/articles/investing/121213/gdp-and-its-importance.asp

Proud Right Winger, retrieved August 1, 2019 https://proudrightwinger.com/blogs/opinion-pieces/5-republican-change-makers

Ross, Chuck "Protesters Gather Outside Mitch McConnell's Home. One Calls For Senator To Break His Neck." Daily Caller August

6, 2019 https://dailycaller.com/2019/08/06/protester-mitch-mcconnell-violence/

Rouse, Martha, U.S Department of Health and Human Services (HHS) "Guide to healthcare compliance resources and agencies." retrieved on June 7, 2018 https://searchhealthit.techtarget.com/definition/Health-and-Human-ServicesHHS

Senior Staff, Press Room, "Betty DeVos, Secretary of Education – Biography, June 27, 2019 https://www2.ed.gov/news/staff/bios/devos.html

Shapiro, William E. The Young People's Encyclopedia of the United States, Vol. 1, Abernathy / Folsom Culture, 1992

Shapiro, William E. The Young People's Encyclopedia of the United States, Vol. 2, Abernathy / Folsom Culture, 1992

Shapiro, William E. The Young People's Encyclopedia of the United States, Vol. 3, Abernathy / Folsom Culture, 1992

SkyNews 2016 https://news.sky.com/story/donald-trumps-election-victory-speech-full-transcript-10651128

The Center on Generational Kinetics "Generational Breakdown Info About All of the Generations." retrieved July 20,2018 https://genhq.com/faq-info-about-generations/

Thegatewaypundit.com, "Complete List of President Trumps Historic Accomplishments." Retrieved on August 5, 2019 https://worldtruth.tv/complete-list-of-president-trumps-historic-accomplishments/

Trump, Ivanka, "Ivanka Trump Bio", Married BiographyDecember 18, 2019 https://marriedbiography.com/ivanka-trump-biography/

Vitali, Ali, "Trump Signs Religious-Liberty Executive Order Allowing For Broad Exemptions", NBC News September 25, 2019 https://www.nbcnews.com/news/us-news/trump-signs-religious-liberty-executive-order-allowing-broad-exemptions-n754786

Warren, Steve, "5 Shocking Facts About New Illinois Late-Term Abortion Law Called 'Death Penalty' For Viable Babies", CBNNEWS.COM, June 12, 2019 https://www1.cbn.com/cbnnews/us/2019/june/5-shocking-facts-about-new-illinois-late-term-abortion-law-called-death-penalty-for-viable-babies

Wattree, Eric L., "We Must Never Confuse Education With Intelligence", March 3, 2013 https://wattree.blogspot.com/2013/03/beneath-spin-eric-l.html

White House, "Melania Trump" https://www.whitehouse.gov/people/melania-trump/

Wikipedia, retrieved August 1, 2019 https://en.wikipedia.org/wiki/Rosie_the_Riveter#Homages

References

Wyrich, Andrew, "Millennials and Gen-Xers now have more voting power than older Americans, study finds". The Daily Dot July 31, 2017 https://www.dailydot.com/layer8/millennials-vote-2016-election/